·FOLK·ART·

THE BEAMISH COLLECTIONS

East hetton Disaster. May. 6th 1897

Rosemary E Allan

First published in 2008 by

Beamish Museum Ltd,
Regional Resource Centre, Beamish,
Co. Durham. DH9 0RG

Registered Charity no. 1122366

Photography by
Rosemary E. Allan, Justin Battong,
Paul Castrey, Duncan Davis, Julian Harrop,
Jim Lawson, Peter Richardson and
Eddie Ryle-Hodges

Design by Ian Brown Design Ltd.

Printed in England by Elanders

British Library Cataloguing in
Publication Data.

A catalogue record for this book is
available from the British Library.

ISBN 0-905054-13-1

The Tanfield ploughman (above)
Artist unknown
(probably copied from a photograph by C. Reid of Wishaw)
c. 1910
Oil on canvas
BM ref. 1979-347.2
190 x 390mm (7$\frac{1}{2}$ x 15$\frac{1}{4}$in)

East Hetton Disaster 6th May 1897 (previous page)
S. Galloway (miner)
after1897
Oil on board
BM ref. 1973-540.1
63 x 49.2mm (25 x 19$\frac{1}{4}$in)

Thomas Ramsay (known as Craky Tommy) (front cover)
Francis Oughton of Pelton Fell
c. 1880
Oil on board
BM ref. 1999-86
55.5 x 42.7mm (22 x 17in)

CONTENTS

Old Miner with lamp and pick
This is a fragment from the original banner from
Page Bank Miners' Lodge, South Brancepeth,
Co. Durham which has subsequently been
over- painted.
Artist unknown
After1884
Oil on fabric

BM ref. 1965-9
1450 x 790mm (57 x 31in)

North Country artist, Ralph Hedley (1848-1913) painted the original 'Geordie Ha'ad the Bairn' in 1890. 'Geordie' was based on Snowdon Pyle, a hewer from North Elswick Colliery. The painting was issued as a print by the Newcastle Weekly Chronicle and became one of the most popular North Country images.

This naïve copy of the painting attempts to emulate the style of the original. Note the proggy mat on the floor and the fender made from an old waggon wheel. On the wall hangs a print of Hedley's painting, illustrating two pitmen 'Going Home', a picture which could be seen in many a pit cottage. The perspective of the fireplace has gone somewhat awry in the translation. This traditional scene could only have been painted in the North of England.

Geordie Ha'ad the Bairn, Artist unknown, after Ralph Hedley, c.1900-10, Oil on canvas,
BM ref. 1994-70.1, 56.1 x 46.2mm (22 x 18in)

INTRODUCTION

'In essence, folk art is the practical creative element in the lives of ordinary working people. It springs from a human reaction to the total physical and social environment, rather than the mainstream artistic culture of Western Europe. It came into being specifically to meet basic human needs, such as safety and security, for which it developed a whole series of signs and symbols which ensured that protection and good fortune sprang from Christian and pre-Christian beliefs. It provided a physical means of expressing joy, love and mourning. It gave its makers an enormous source of satisfaction, allowing them to display their skill and inventiveness to the full.'

Peter Brears, North Country Folk Art. 1989

THE VERY TERM 'FOLK ART' defies description. 'Naïve art', 'primitive art', 'popular art', 'people's art' and even 'working class art' are all terms that have been used to describe it, though all have differing meanings and connotations.

Folk Art is very much the art of the individual; it embodies the ideas, skills and creativity of the maker as well as the need to make something of use and often of beauty. It sometimes harks back to an older understood tradition passed down to younger generations, or can be of a new form adapting new materials to an old use. It possesses a freedom of its own, and is not bound by academic convention, even though it might be influenced by it. Its maker has, in many cases, taken great pride and spent many precious leisure hours in its production. It represents a part of his life, thoughts and identity, uniquely his own.

Symbolism is sometimes used as a separate language within Folk Art to convey specific meanings. The true lover's knot, hearts and baskets can symbolise love, happiness and fruitfulness. The symbolic devices of clasped hands often refer to the motto 'Unity is Strength', whilst the beehive with its busy bees, stands for industry and co-operation. The figure of Liberty signifies freedom and the wheatsheaf stands for plenty and abundance. The old Craft Guilds had their own emblems, from which Masonic symbolism developed.

Pieces of folk art were often utilitarian in nature and served the purposes and needs of the household. A chimney crane made by the local blacksmith would be ornamented with extra flourishes; a spoon rack was carefully designed to be both useful and decorative with its inlays; a gansey was knitted for warmth and protection against the elements but also demonstrated a particular pattern of stitches known to the wearer; the seat of a Windsor chair was shaped from a single piece of wood to fit the shape of the user, and the knitting sheath, although made for use, was also a symbol of love with its inscriptions and decoration! The materials, from which folk art was fashioned, were often left-over fabric, scraps of metal or brass 'rescued' from the works or even waste material in the form of cigarette packets, cows' horns, or pieces of old bone!

Folk Art was also the product, not only of the individual but also of the community in which that individual lived and worked. The close nature of the pit village communities of the North, for instance, inspired a particular form and strength of expression. A long tradition, together with a sense of dependence of the individual each upon another, sometimes to the point of life and death, reinforced the need to create something of beauty, which could be appreciated at the time, and which could be passed on and treasured by future generations. Such is the wonderful diversity of Folk Art – an important but sadly neglected part of our cultural heritage.

PAINTINGS *Shorthorn - The Teeswater Ox*

THIS OIL PAINTING of a 'Teeswater Ox' is a rare survival, being one of the earliest representations of a Teeswater / Shorthorn of c. 1780/1790, painted whilst still 'unimproved', and by an 'artist' who had received little or no formal training. From about 1780, a new scientific approach and interest in agriculture led to a revolution in livestock breeding techniques, and consequently it was at this period that the painting of farm animals became fashionable. Paintings were commissioned by owners and breeders, not only to impress their friends and clients, but also to publicise to the world at large, the success of the new breeding and of their stock in particular. Animal portraiture became respectable and the work of highly competent professional painters. The tradition continued until about 1880, when painted portraits were largely replaced by photography.

The Shorthorn breed was the first to establish its own herd book in 1822, tracing records of all known blood lines. The breed predominated in the North of England and even before the pioneering and improving work of the Colling brothers, Shorthorns were renowned for their size.

Oil on canvas, Artist unknown, c.1775-80
BM ref. 2001-12, 635 x 740mm (25 x 29in)

hestnut Arabian imported into England by Fitzhugh Esq. the property of Mr. Chas. Willson

Chestnut Arabian

Arabian horses were first brought into England from the Middle East in the early 17th century. They were imported as the only pure breed or thoroughbred to improve our native stock and they played a major part in the development of the British Thoroughbred, our racehorse. The breed was noted for its spirit, intelligence and stamina. Imported horses were often named after their owners, who took a tremendous pride in them. This watercolour is inscribed *'Chestnut Arabian imported into England by Fitzhugh Esq. the property of Mr. Chas. Willson'*. The Arabian, although the property of Willson, was brought into England by the Earl of Kinoul,

Ambassador at Constantinople, where he cost over £2001.

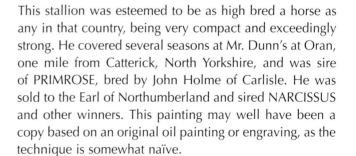

This stallion was esteemed to be as high bred a horse as any in that country, being very compact and exceedingly strong. He covered several seasons at Mr. Dunn's at Oran, one mile from Catterick, North Yorkshire, and was sire of PRIMROSE, bred by John Holme of Carlisle. He was sold to the Earl of Northumberland and sired NARCISSUS and other winners. This painting may well have been a copy based on an original oil painting or engraving, as the technique is somewhat naïve.

Chestnut Arabian, Artist unknown, after J.Wootton (1678-1765), Mid 18th century, Watercolour on paper
BM ref. 1991-270, 273 x 198mm (10¾ x 7¾ in)

A Clydesdale Horse

The stallion depicted here, by the name of 'Hewson' was exported by John Kerr of Wigton, Cumbria, to the Lafayette Stock Farm, founded by Jeptha Crouch, at Lafayette, Indiana, USA, the largest stock importer of fine horses in the USA. The Americans were so delighted with 'Hewson' that they had a painting made by HENRY DOUSA to send to the Kerr family. The artist, Dousa is believed to have been born c.1820, though his national origin is unclear, as apparently he had applied for US citizenship in 1882, stating that he was a native of France. Between 1879 and 1885, he worked in Newcastle, Indiana. He had a particular interest in animal portraiture, unusual at that time in the USA and more associated with British folk painting. Dousa was a self taught painter known for his farm scenes and prizewinning livestock, later turning to portraiture. His paintings are all similar in concept and show the animals in profile against a green background. The painting has a primitive charm, which was fashionable in America though possibly not so well understood in Britain. (The painting was discovered in the 1980s, rolled up on the wall plate of a farm barn, just as it had originally been sent!) It is probable that the taste of Cumbrian horse breeders was unlike that of their American counterparts, as this painting represents the finest of American folk art. The Kerr family lived at Red Hall Farm from 1863 and continued to breed pedigree heavy horses until the early 1950s.

Oil on canvas, Henry Dousa (c.1820-1891), 1891
BM ref. 1980-481.6, 880 x 610mm (34½ x 24in)

Watercolour on paper (bound album) Family Annals, By Road and Rail, By Flood and Field.
'On the High Level Bridge – A Sudden Reversion' Newcastle upon Tyne. c.1880, Samuel Tuke Richardson (1846-1904)
BM ref. 1991-385, 420 x 230mm (16¹/₂ x 9in)

Samuel Tuke Richardson's Watercolours

SAMUEL TUKE RICHARDSON (1846-1904), 'coachman and artist extraordinaire', was born into a prominent Quaker family in Sunderland. His father was Edward Richardson, who was related to the Backhouse family, the well known bankers. In 1873, Samuel worked as a bank clerk at Backhouse's Bank in Darlington, though his main passion in life was for horses and carriage driving. His superb sketch books and journals reveal a wonderful sense of humour as well as an extensive knowledge of carriage driving, emphasising the many dangers of travelling by coach in the 19th century. During his lifetime, Samuel published several works which illustrate his sketches and stories including *The Friends in Council* of 1875 and *The World's First Railway Jubilee* of 1876. All are full of wit and sarcasm!

Illustrations from two hitherto unpublished works in the Beamish collections are seen here. *Family Annals, by Road and Rail, by Flood* and *Field* and *Our Drive to Albalanda.* Both books give wonderful accounts of travelling the roads by coach.

Watercolour on paper (bound album) Our Drive to Albalanda. 'Leaving our kind hostess at Derwent Lodge' Shotley Bridge, Co. Durham.
c.1901-2, Samuel Tuke Richardson, (1846-1904)
BM ref. 1999-135, 380 x 270mm (15 x 10³/₄in)

Remember the Poor Old Horses

This painting is entitled *Early Days of the Steam Train*, though it appears to have been inspired by a cartoon of the period bemoaning the *Effects of the Railroad on the Brute Creation*, dating c.1831. Opponents of the new railroads claimed that they would put an end to all road traffic! The painting illustrates a landscape with the Liverpool and Manchester railway in the background. In the foreground, the redundant coach horses, endeavouring to earn a living, have formed a musical trio with collecting boxes highly visible. The coopered bucket bears a label, 'Remember the Poor Old Horses'. The carthorses in the field beyond are suffering from starvation and showing their ribs and one stands at the Corn Warehouse with an empty bucket waiting to be fed.

Early Days of the Steam Train, Artist unknown, 1838, Oil on canvas
BM ref. 1994-191,   450 x 380mm (17³⁄₄ x 15in)

The Steam Elephant

Full size working replica of the Steam Elephant loco in operation at Beamish (right).

One of the museum's most exciting recent discoveries was an oil painting of a very early locomotive of c.1815. The locomotive set into a landscape is reminiscent of many of the animal portraits undertaken at the same period. Exhaustive researches undertaken by museum staff have highlighted the significance and importance of this lost locomotive, and have enabled detailed design drawings to be made prior to the rebuilding of a replica of this engine.

The engine, known as *The Steam Elephant*, was one of the pioneering locomotives of the North East of England. It was designed by William Chapman, a civil engineer based in Newcastle upon Tyne, who worked closely with John Buddle, the greatest of the colliery engineers or viewers, known as *The King of the Coal Trade*. Their first locomotive was built in 1813 for Heaton Colliery and this was followed by another for the Lambton Collieries in 1814. This painting is of an engine built c.1814/1815 for Wallsend Colliery, with machined parts made by Hawks' Foundry of Gateshead. Built for the specific purpose of pulling heavy loads of coal up steep inclines, its first trials on wooden track appear to have been unsuccessful; however, when the rails were transferred to iron, it worked well for a number of years. In 1828, Buddle writing to Lord Londonderry mentions that 'The Steam Elephant takes his station today...'

The Steam Elephant, Oil on canvas, Artist unknown, 1815
920 x 610mm (36 x 24in)

Crow Trees Colliery

CROW TREES COLLIERY, near Quarrington Hill, Co. Durham, was sunk in the early 1830s, the first cargo of coal being shipped at Stockton, at the Clarence Railway Staithes on board the brig *Etherley* for London. The colliery was owned by Messrs. William Hedley & Sons and it is thought that the figure on the grey horse is that of William Hedley, himself. The two locomotives illustrated are both four wheelers, possibly *Exile*, built by Nesham and Welsh in 1838 and *Tyneside* built by R. & W. Hawthorn in 1836. The colliery was owned by William Hedley until 1837/8.

JAMES WOOD practised as an artist in Newcastle in the early 19th century. He became known for his street scenes with small figures, many featuring the older buildings of the city. He was also known as a painter of portrait miniatures and much of his work was small in scale. His accuracy and attention to detail is illustrated particularly well in this painting, which could almost be said to consist of a series of vignettes. The horse gin with the school of children and see-saw detail is quite charming. It is not known whether James Wood painted many colliery scenes, though a very similar painting by him does exist of this colliery, and it may be that he was commissioned by William Hedley to paint the colliery for members of the family. James Wood died apparently in reduced circumstances in Newcastle in 1886.

Crow Trees Colliery, Co. Durham, James Wood (signed and dated), April 1841, Oil on canvas
BM ref. 2007-235, 356 x 530mm (14 x 21in)

Wearmouth Colliery

The sinking of WEARMOUTH COLLIERY, (known later as Monkwearmouth), began in 1826, and the pit opened in June 1835. The seams of coal were of excellent quality and the Bensham seam was recorded as being 5ft 8ins thick. In 1834, at 1720ft deep, this mine was 'the deepest mine in the world'. It is related that Mr. Pemberton, the owner, was told that, owing to the great depth which he had caused to be sunk, he would never find coal there. 'Ah, well' he said, 'then we'll dig to Hell and find cinders.' By 1894 the mine was employing 2000 men and boys and its daily output was 2000 tons.

Miners have always felt a need to express themselves whether through their paintings, poetry, songs or sporting activities. This somewhat naïve watercolour of Wearmouth Colliery from the South West seems to be an accurate representation of a pithead scene of the period.

Wearmouth Colliery closed on Nov.24th 1993, and the site was redeveloped by Sunderland Football Club to house their new, Stadium of Light - a veritable case of 'from out of darkness there came light'. The name is supposed to be a reference to the miners' lamp and indeed many of Sunderland's football supporters previously worked in the mines of the region.

Wearmouth Colliery, R. Kane, 1879, Watercolour
BM ref. 1973-267, 530 x 397mm (21 x 15½in)

Philadelphia, R. Young (signed and dated), 1899, Oil on canvas
BM ref. 1986-103, 407 x 707mm (18³/₄ x 30¹/₂ in)

Pit Cottages at Philadelphia, Co. Durham

The colliery at Philadelphia, sometimes known as New Herrington, Co. Durham, was sunk in 1874 and worked until 1985. In the Great Northern Coalfield of Northumberland and Durham, houses, built by the Coal Companies, were provided for the miners, free in exchange for work, however if the miner was injured and could not work, the family could be evicted from the house. The painting illustrates two rows of cottages, the older single storey row on the right being built of magnesium limestone with a later brick pantry outshot and roof of pantiles. The window shutters on these houses were a distinct feature enabling blackout and taking into account the different shifts which the pitman worked. When a pit was sunk, the stone removed from the shaft was used for building the first row of houses, as close to the pit as was possible. This first row was often called Sinkers' Row or Stone Row. Later houses were usually built of brick with

slate roofs. It was customary for the houses at the ends of the rows to be larger and these would be occupied by the officials.

In the painting, the pit head can be seen just beyond the houses and children play in the street. Broken bricks litter the street of black ash and hens scavenge for food. Pitmen took great pride in their dogs and in the foreground several can be seen contemplating a fight! The painting, with its cotton wool clouds is certainly naïve in style, but it has captured the essence of a typical pit village in its attention to detail.

Miners from Billy Row, near Crook, Co. Durham
with prize winning whippet, c.1911,
BM ref. 23073

A filler at Bedlington 'A' Harvey Seam. - 'Well this one is Craddock; he had the world record for filling coal. I cannot recall off hand, but it's in the records how many tons he filled in a day and it was fantastic mind what he shifted.'
James MacKenzie, 1970s/80s, Oil on board, BM ref. 1993-27.12, 485 x 385mm (19 x 15¼ in)

Oil Paintings by James Mackenzie

JAMES MACKENZIE was born on 21st September 1927 at Bedlington Station in Northumberland. His father was a coal miner and his mother worked in the local brickworks. One of his earliest memories was of seeing his father being brought home with terrible injuries, on a horse drawn coal cart. The family moved to Barrington Colliery, when James was 5 years old, and at school he began to show early signs of an artistic temperament. He took up painting and his sketch book went everywhere with him. His first job, at the age of 14, was on the heapstead at the Bedlington 'A' pit, and it was here that he found inspiration for many of his paintings of pit life and the pit communities. Although he worked in a variety of styles using different materials, these particular works were inspired by the Ashington School of Painters of which MacKenzie was a member in the 1970s and 1980s. He attended evening classes at King's College, Newcastle to develop his style, and after serving in the army from 1945 as regimental sign writer, took up sign writing as a job on demobilisation, never returning to mining.

Mr F Taylor with his prize winning leeks, Pittington Co-op Leek Show 1955.
BM ref. 67826

Handling and Preparing Leeks on Show Day, Barrington Colliery. - 'It's really a fine art, and it's January when you put them in and they are reared in the greenhouse. About April or May they plant them out in the garden then and they're special, they're into selective breeding. There was all these, if you had a good leek, that's the one you seeded the next year.'
James MacKenzie, 1970s/80s, Oil on board, BM ref. 1993-27.7, 485 x 385 mm (19 x 15¼ in)

Thomas Ramsey

THOMAS RAMSEY has been described by John Wilson, one of the Durham leaders, in his *History of the Durham Miners' Association* as *'a most perfect type of old school miner and a sound Trade Unionist, one of the heroes of '44. With bills under his arm and a crake in hand, he went from row to row announcing meetings and urging the men to attend. His words were few but forcible; not polished but very pointed – and they went home. "Lads, unite and better your condition. When eggs are scarce, eggs are dear; when men are scarce, men are dear"... he was never afraid to stand up before his brethren and agitate for that amelioration in the condition of the working pitmen, which has at length been conceded. His style of oratory was gifted with a warmth of expression and his perfect knowledge of the one subject he engaged upon – the danger and the excessive toil of the miner's life - caused him to be held in respect by masters and men alike.'*

Ramsey organised the Pitmen's Union with Thomas Hepburn in 1831. The 1860s were regarded as a stormy epoch, though the basis for trade unionism emerged in Durham from the agitation of this period. Tommy Ramsey was a 'blacklisted' miner, a 'sacrificed man', who did much to further the cause of unionism leading to the formation of the lodges of the Durham Miners' Association, in 1869. He died on 8th May 1873 at the age of 62, and was buried at Blaydon. The painting has a haunting quality about it which has captured the very essence of the man with his steely eyes and strong determination to achieve his goal.

Thomas Ramsay – Craky Tommy, Francis Oughton, Date not known, Oil on board
BM ref. 1999-86, 555 x 427mm (22 x 17in)

Watercolours by Oswald Bage

OSWALD BAGE (1907-1963) was born at Leadgate, near Consett, Co. Durham. From a mining family, Oswald left school at fourteen years old, to work in the colliery at Consett. In 1925 his first published drawing appeared in the *North Mail*. The under manager of the colliery had caught him 'fooling around one day' sketching in chalk on a piece of old iron. He immediately recognised the lad's talents and made sure that he received some tuition from local artist Frederick Davison. From 1940-1945, Oswald served with the RAF, continuing to paint and undertake special commissions for the US Marine Corps. After the war, he returned to work at the Consett Iron Company and, whilst fitter's mate in the fitting shops, painted many industrial scenes, such as the watercolours illustrated here. In 1946 with friends, he had re-formed The Consett Art Group, setting up a junior section. Teaching became a major interest and he continued to teach until his early death in 1963.

The Forging Shop (above) - Consett Iron Company, Oswald Bage, 1946, Watercolour BM ref. 1984-42.4, 294 x 236mm (11^1/$_2$ x 9^1/$_4$ in)

The Blacksmith's Shop (below) - Consett Iron Company, Oswald Bage, 1950, Watercolour BM ref. 1984-42.2, 493 x 320mm (19^1/$_2$ x 12^1/$_2$ in)

Mary Alice Oliver

This delightful picture was discovered as a very black canvas blocking up the fireplace of a bedroom in Durham City! When cleaned, it revealed the portrait of Mary Alice Oliver, born on August 31st 1847 and aged nine years old when the painting was done.

The sitter is placed in three-quarters pose, in a rural landscape, emulating the work of the professional painter. Whilst the painting of the figure here lacks detail, appearing to be rather flat and unfinished, overall the portrait has a naïve charm, which still manages to capture the youthful essence of the sitter. It was customary for fashionable artists to paint their subjects with a family pet and that tradition has been maintained here.

Mary Alice Oliver, Artist unknown, c.1856, Oil on canvas
BM ref. 1987-228.21, 914 x 710mm (36 x 28in)

TRADITIONAL FURNITURE

Spoon rack

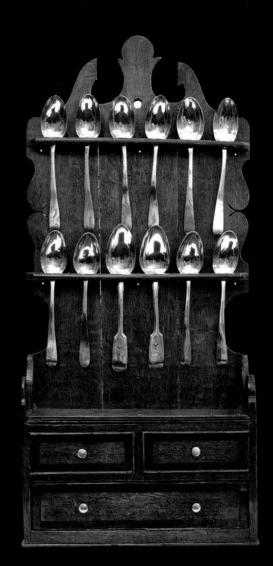

SPOON RACKS were often used in farmhouses and cottages for storing the cutlery. The spoons, because of their more delicate nature, were stored separately and were displayed brightly polished in racks. The drawers below were used for the heavier knives and forks. This example is in oak with drawers cross-banded in mahogany. The smaller drawers are dummies and are accessed from a sliding panel above. Because of their basic construction, these small domestic pieces could be home made and were often embellished with scrolls and fancy shapes. This spoon rack from Rothbury in Northumberland is a typical provincial country piece.

Spoon Rack, Maker not known, 1810-30
Oak cross banded with mahogany
BM ref. 2008-1, 344 x 745mm (13^1/$_2$ x 29 ^{1}/$_2$ in)

Long Case Clock

Painted or 'enamelled' dialled clocks were introduced from the 1770s onwards. They were colourful, easy to read and new, and quickly became as popular, in country farmhouses and cottages as in wealthier town houses and mansions. They were more expensive than clocks with brass dials, which rapidly went out of fashion.

The maker of this clock, RALPH WESTON II, (1760-1812) came from a family of clock makers working in Weardale from 1750 until 1836. Whilst the majority of scenes painted in the arches of these new white dialled clocks are purely imaginary, the dial of this clock is remarkable in that it represents an actual scene entitled 'View of a Coal engine on the River Tyne

with a Pit at work'. A typical colliery scene, chaldron waggons and coal carts are clustered around a horse gin with adjoining pump house and ventilation structures, whilst the background shows a panoramic view of Newcastle with a Tyne keel sailing up the river.

The top of the arch is even more remarkable in that it features an advert for the dial maker, 'Sold only by Beilby and Hawthorn, Newcastle'. This is of course William Beilby, the glass engraver who had been associated with Thomas Bewick. Beilby and Hawthorn were the only dial makers working in the North East between 1797 and 1817, when Beilby died.

Eight day Long Case Clock, Maker not known, c.1820-30, Case of mahogany
BM ref. 2004-98, 2100mm (83in) high Dial 360mm (14in)

Long Case Clock

Painted dials became popular from the late 18th century and remained so right up until 1870/80, when they ceased to be fashionable. Many of the dials featured allegorical scenes of cattle, cottage and landscape, in stark contrast to the reality of the life of the rural labourer.

The most popular folk hero, Robert Burns was often shown as Burns at the Plough, as can be seen here. The four corners of the dial illustrate the four countries, England, Scotland, Ireland and Wales. From the 1820s, these clocks were frequently painted in luminous and bold colours, true to the folk tradition. The distinctive long hood was often to be found in clocks from the West of Scotland, though this clock came from Wooler, in Northumberland, on the Borders.

Press cupboard
Maker not known
c. 1680-90
Oak
BM ref. 1975-143
1690 x 1660 x 560mm
(66¹/₂ x 65¹/₂ x 22in)

A North East Court Cupboard

Press cupboards, sometimes known as court cupboards, were a prominent feature in late 16th and early 17th century houses. They were used, usually in the dining area to store utensils, pewter wares, crockery and sometimes food for the household. In some areas, particularly the Lake District, these cupboards were built into alcoves or formed room dividers. Recent research has identified a style of carving from the North East of England in both wainscot chairs and press cupboards. The design incorporates a stylised 'tree of life' and a diamond pattern. According to family tradition, this cupboard belonged to Roger Heaton of South Acton Farm, near Felton in Northumberland. He died c.1803 and the cupboard passed down in the family.

Windsor Chair

Windsor Chair is a term used for chairs with a wooden seat, with back uprights mortised into it and with legs mortised from below. The early 18th century saw the trade in these chairs centred on High Wycombe, although chairs of this type were made, with regional variations all round the country. Local craftsmen made use of the materials and tools to hand, producing their own individual styles. This rocking chair is certainly one of these. The rockers project much further at the back than the front, though the balance and design of the chair have been thoughtfully worked out.

The seat has been carefully shaped from one piece of wood, to create the most comfortable and sturdy chair which fits all sizes! Even though the timber in the seat has twisted, it is a superb example of country craftsmanship.

The chair was purchased for 2/6d, from the farm sale of T.J. Alderson at Three Chimneys Farm, Spital, near Bowes, Co. Durham, in 1962.

Spindle Backed Rocking Chair, Maker not known, c.1860-1880, Ash
BM ref. 1962-235, 1090 x 600 mm (43^1/$_2$ x 23^1/$_2$in)

Spinning Wheel
Jonathan Garbut
c.1800
Fruitwood

BM ref. 2003-113.1
990 x 695mm (39 x 27¹/₂ in)

TEXTILES

Spinning Wheel
and Wool Winder

EXTILES were not a principal industry of the North East region as a whole, although in South Durham, Darlington had become a nationally important centre for the production of linen from flax. The carpet industry also flourished in Barnard Castle and in Durham City.

Carding and spinning of wool was an occupation which could be carried out in the home, producing spun wool for knitting, and at the same time provided extra income for the household. Flax could also be spun on the same wheels as wool, ready to be woven into bed linen and shirting.

Both spinning wheel and wool winder were made by JONATHAN GARBUT of Stockton on Tees. Jonathan is listed as a turner in the 1796 Directory and also in the Directory of 1811 as turner and wheelwright. The wool winder bears the words *Turn me Right or I'm broke Quite* and also the name *Jonathan Garbut Maker Stockton*. Both pieces illustrate similar turned sections.

Wool winder
Jonathan Garbut
c.1800
Fruitwood

BM ref. 2003-113.2
945 x 695mm (37¹/₄ x 27¹/₂ in)

Samplers

The earliest known surviving sampler was made in 1598. Samplers were an aide memoire to learning and recording stitches and patterns. They illustrate the different stages that a girl would have progressed through to acquire the necessary needlework skills.

From the mid 17th century alphabets were used when the making of samplers became part of a school's curriculum. They taught embroidery stitches as well as elementary literacy. Many 18th century samplers were worked with religious texts, reflecting the influence of John Wesley and the Methodist Movement.

DOROTHY MAFFIN, aged 10, embroidered the Ten Commandments on her sampler (right) at Tynemouth Workhouse in 1810.

ELIZABETH GREEN worked this Memorial sampler (right) c.1890, recording the dates of deaths and burials of members of the same family.

ELIZABETH BROWN of Newcastle upon Tyne 'worked this in the 17th year of her Age' in 1844. She later married Thomas Hindmarsh of Newburn in 1864. The initials may well be those of her parents. Solomon's Temple is surrounded by other popular motifs of sailing ship, birds, flowers and windmill, framed by an outer border of stylised flowers.

BM ref. 1991-205, 510 x 455mm (20 x 18in)

BM ref. 1991-184, 790 x 610mm (31 x 24in)

BM ref. 1978-541.1, 820 x 750mm (32¹/₄ x 29¹/₂ in

Patchwork and Appliqué Quilt

The history of quilts and quilting in the North of England can be traced back to the 15th century, the craft reflecting the social and cultural conditions in which the quilts were made. Essentially a thrift craft, many were produced as bed quilts or petticoats to be worn by country folk. Some were made by the pitman's wife to earn a livelihood in hard times and others were made for weddings and special occasions and are superb examples of folk art.

This wedding quilt, made c.1815-30 in Weardale, Co. Durham, exhibits all the symbolism of love, prosperity and fruitfulness, in its patchwork and appliqué design. White hearts are set on a red background and baskets of flowers predominate.

Early Hearts Quilt, Maker not known, 1815-30, Pieced and applied printed cottons
BM ref. 1990-282, 2700 x 2500mm (106 x 98in)

Hooky Rug, Maker not known though made at Fourstones, Northumberland, c.1916, Wool rags BM ref. 1996-115, 1570 x 735mm (62 x 29in)

Rag Rugs

The origins of rag rug making are obscure, though it is thought that the craft came from Scandinavia, arriving in Britain around the late 1400s. Rag rugs were made in all parts of the country, being known by a variety of names including bodgy, broddy, clippy, clooty, hooky, proggy, proddy, peggy, stobby, or tabby, according to whichever part of the country you were in!

The craft demonstrates recycling at its best. Old clothes, stockings, blankets, uniforms and suits are cut up into clippings ready to go into the mat. There are two basic types of rag rug; the hooky is worked from the front and long pieces of material are hooked through a hessian backing to form the pattern; the proggy is worked from the back and here shorter pieces of material are poked through to form a short pile on the right side of the mat.

The craft was carried on from necessity, originally in working class households, which could not afford machine made floor coverings. They were never considered respectable enough to be included in the many needlework magazines of the Victorian period. The rugs provided not only comfort and colour, but also kept rooms cosy, taking away the chill of stone floors. They were therefore functional as well as attractive, many being masterpieces of design and real works of art.

*Hooky Rug
Maker not known
Early 1900s
Wool rags and
old blankets*

*BM ref.
1994-42.3
1520 x 840mm
(60 x 33in)*

The Hexham Builders' Trade Banner

Early trade banners were usually the work of anonymous craftsmen with a background in sign writing, house painting or coach painting. The early craft based societies used the ancient symbolism, emblems and mottos of their trade to emphasise their historic lineage, tradition and respectability. As the early craft societies combined, they became stronger and the banners reflect the purpose of the early unions in striving for unity, strength, justice and industry. These banners have a vibrancy and originality that the later banners have lost.

This banner has an inscription *Builders' Society Hexham* and dates to c.1830-40. It represents the builders' trade in every aspect incorporating the arms of the Masons, the Glaziers, the Blacksmiths, the Plasterers and Bricklayers, and Slaters and Tylers. The arms and mottos are very similar to those illustrated in *The Arms of the Several Companies in the Corporation of Newcastle upon Tyne* of 1776, and their significance would have been well recognised throughout the country.

Hexham Trade Banner, Artist not known, c.1830-40, Oil paint on cotton
BM ref. 2006-219, 2660 x 2260mm (105 x 89 in)

Miners' Lodge Banner

The banners of the Great Northern Coalfield, in many ways symbolise the history and traditions of an industry, now gone, through the struggle for workers' rights, social justice and fair pay. The banners were carried, at the Durham Miners' Gala, the Northumberland Miners' Picnic, during major strikes and rallies and were also used at social events and funerals. They sum up the aspirations of the miners through mottos such as *United We Stand, Unity is Strength, Emancipation of Labour* and *The Sunshine of Liberty*. Many used allegorical scenes to portray their messages.

After 1837, many banners were made by the firm of George Tutill of London. George had started life as a travelling showman working in fairgrounds painting fascias and signage. He developed a technique of making double sided banners, oil painted onto silk, by using a coating of India rubber. The silk was woven into ornate patterns on the largest Jacquard looms in the world.

The banner of the West Stanley Lodge depicts a scene from the catastrophic disaster which occurred in 1909. 168 men and boys were killed when the Burns Pit exploded. In the underground scene, a scroll is inscribed *The Unknown Miner*, whilst above ground, houses and gardens are illustrated next to the pit and above an angel carries an olive branch. The banner, with its unique picture, was created as a memorial to the disaster, and as a reminder of the constant dangers of mining.

West Stanley Miners' Lodge Banner, Co. Durham, Artist unknown, made by Tutill of London, c. 1920s, Oil painted onto silk
BM ref. 1984-10.27, 3040 x 2540mm (134 x 100in)

Gansey in navy wool
Maker not known
c. 1900
Seahouses,
Northumberland
BM ref. 1980-855.4

Detail of Gansey in green wool
Made by Mrs. Libby Grant
c.1900
Eyemouth, Berwickshire
BM ref. 1979-869

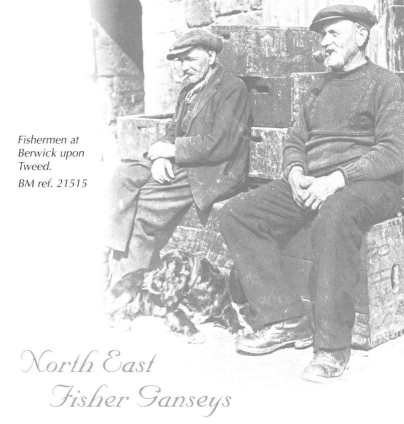

Fishermen at
Berwick upon
Tweed.
BM ref. 21515

North East Fisher Ganseys

The first record of knitted goods being manufactured for sale in the British Isles appeared in the 15th century. Hand knitting became an important cottage industry which survived, well into the 19th century, even after the introduction of knitting frames. It persisted, in the more isolated Dales, in the Lake District, and in the country areas of Yorkshire, Northumberland and Durham, well into the 20th century.

In the fishing communities, of the north east coast, the knitting of socks and 'ganseys' continued, the close-knitted traditional patterns giving an element of protection and warmth to the seaman's seamless pullover. Patterns, originally used for stockings, were translated by the fishwives into ganseys, and individual designs became associated with particular families and places. The knitter, using a knitting sheath to support the curved metal needle, would work, 'in the round' using a circular technique, an essential feature of the gansey construction. The arms would be knitted down from the shoulder to the cuff, enabling worn parts to be repaired more easily.

TRADITIONAL WOODCARVINGS

Knitting Sheaths

AMONGST smaller domestic utensils, fashioned from wood and sometimes known as 'treen', the knitting sheath is one of the most interesting and attractive. The technique of knitting is slow though the knitting sheath helped to speed it up. Worn on the right-hand side of the body between the waist and the arm pit, it held a needle, which supported the knitting, releasing the fingers of the right hand for throwing the wool. Knitting sheaths were normally made from many different types of wood, in a multitude of shapes and sizes, though examples are also found in brass, bone, glass, silver and even bunches of straw or horsehair. Often elaborately carved and embellished, they were given as love-tokens by young men to their sweethearts. The magnificent sheath, with open lantern, loose balls and wooden chain, was carved from one piece of wood, by TIMOTHY TARN of Woolpits Hill, Ettersgill in Teesdale for his cousin's wife, Elizabeth Beadle (nee Scott) of Egg Pot Farm, Forest in Teesdale and was presented to her in May 1892. It was never used for knitting, but kept purely as an ornament!

Above, from top:

Knitting sheath, c. 1800
Fruitwood
BM ref. 2002-171.25
230 mm (9in)

Chip-carved sheath
from Mickleton, Teesdale
BM ref. 1980-522.1
210 mm (8¹/4in)

Very fine chip-carved sheath
Ash, Teesdale area
BM ref. 2002-171.24
195 mm (7³/4in)

Chain Knitting sheath
Made by Timothy Tarn
1892
BM ref. 1980-525.1
420 mm (16¹/2in)

Left:

Sheath in satinwood with
the name of Elizabeth
Thompson, Thornley, 1854
BM ref. 2002-171.1
190 mm (7¹/2in)

Timothy Tarn
BM ref. 19,335

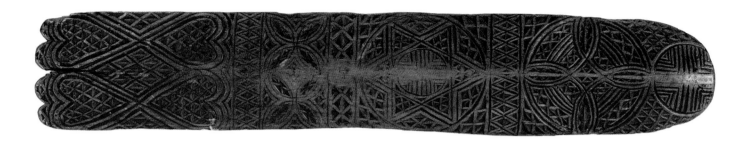

BM ref. 1999-3.60, 320mm (12¹/₂ in)

Stay Busks

The stay busk was another form of carved wooden love-token. The term 'busk' was used to describe a carved piece of wood or bone, which passed down the front of stays or was laced into the front of corsets in order to keep them straight. Used in the Tudor and Elizabethan periods, they survived into the 17th, 18th and early 19th centuries. Stay busks are usually decorated in chip-carving with various geometric designs such as interlocking hearts, circles and flowers. The busk (above) from the Darlington area, is a treasure with a wonderful carved message on the reverse; 'When this you see pray think of me tho many miles we distant be. Tho we are a great way apart I wish you well with all my heart. IC 1783'

Stay busk (above and left) with chip carved hearts and diamonds dated 1791.

BM ref. 2004-114, 320mm (12¹/₂ in)

Carving of a Pitman

The 'Deputy' in the coal mine held an important and responsible position. Having been selected by the Manager, for his above average ability, his job was to examine the main working places, to set timber to support the roof and to examine the safety lamps, making daily reports for the Manager. He could easily be distinguished by his leather skull cap and deputy's stick, used for measuring the seams.

In his *Our Coal and Our Coal Pits* of 1853, J.R.Leifchild wrote of the pitman *'his stature is diminutive, his figure disproportionate and misshapen; his legs being much bowed; his chest protruding. His arms are long, and oddly suspended. His countenance is not less striking than his figure; his cheeks being generally hollow, his brow overhanging, his cheekbones high, his forehead low and retreating; nor is his appearance healthful.'*

This wood carving of a deputy depicts an accurate representation of a northern miner epitomising strength and ruggedness of character.

*Photo (above)
Deputy with miners at
Chester Moor Colliery,
Co. Durham c.1901
BM ref. 68060.*

*Carved wooden figure
of a pitman
Craftsman unknown
Newcastle upon Tyne
c. 1850-1900*

*BM ref. 1980-431
1830 x 600 x 400mm
(72 x 23¹/₂ x 16in).*

Carved Boxes

These small boxes have been beautifully carved from blocks of solid mahogany. Although these examples were all collected from the North of England, the tradition of making such boxes is universal. The boxes have been hollowed out, and sometimes take the shape of a book. A sliding lid is cunningly disguised within the carved design, which includes hearts, rosettes, quadrants and zigzags. The boxes may have been made as love tokens to hold a treasured item and occasionally to house a small mirror.

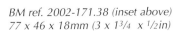

BM ref. 2002-171.38 (inset above)
77 x 46 x 18mm (3 x 1³/4 x ¹/2in)

BM ref. 2002-171.36 (top row right)
108 x 72 x 30mm (4¹/4 x 2³/4 x 1¹/4 in)

BM ref. 2002-171.37 (middle row right)
88 x 71 x 20mm (3¹/2 x 2³/4 x ³/4 in)

BM ref. 2002-171.34 (bottom row right)
70 x 48 x 22mm (2³/4 x 2 x ³/4 in)

Splint work

Splint work was a popular hobby practised throughout the North of England from the 18th century onwards. Thin strips of wood were joined together by means of careful notching and jointing, each piece of wood supporting the next without the use of nails or glue. Sometimes lead shot was enclosed within the joints allowing them to rattle. Picture frames, model chairs and rattles were made in this way as well as other novelty pieces.

In later days, lollipop sticks and old clothes pegs, were saved and recycled into a form of splint work by gluing them together.

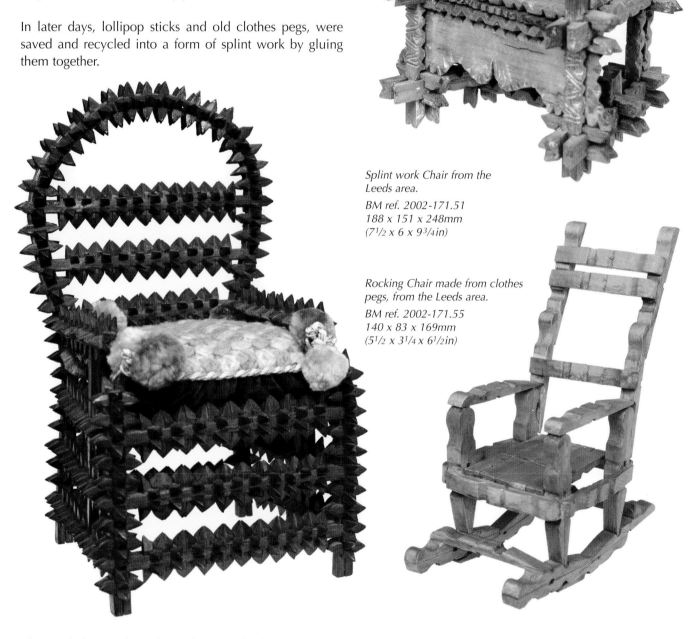

Splint work Chair from the Leeds area.
BM ref. 2002-171.51
188 x 151 x 248mm
(7¹/₂ x 6 x 9³/₄in)

Rocking Chair made from clothes pegs, from the Leeds area.
BM ref. 2002-171.55
140 x 83 x 169mm
(5¹/₂ x 3¹/₄ x 6¹/₂in)

Chair made from a railway sleeper, by a retired railwayman in Rochdale.
Short sharp pointed splints are interlocked around a pair of long flexible splints.
BM ref. 2002-171.52, 240 x 177 x 335mm (9¹/₂ x 7 x 13in)

METALWORK

Copper Weathervane

Weathervane in the shape of a cockerel
Maker not known , c.1862
Weathervane in sheet copper
BM ref. 1989-344.1
740 x 720mm (29 x 28¹/₄in.)

THE COPPERSMITH WAS A SKILLED CRAFTSMAN who worked in sheet copper. His living would be made from making set pots, boilers, pans, lamps and ship's vents as well as from roofing. Weathervanes were both practical and ornamental and allowed him to exhibit his artistry. Change in wind direction was often an important indicator of weather to come, influencing agriculture and other rural activities. The design depended on an attractive and suitable shape, easily seen from a distance. This example bears various inscriptions, including 'R.Shaw 1882', 'J.C.R. 82', 'T.H. May 29 1862', 'W.Dobson', and 'J. Trenham'. 1862 may be its original date of manufacture or could refer, like the other dates to repairs carried out over the years.

Tobacco Box

English tobacco boxes depicting a particular occupation were prized possessions. In this example the brass has been incised with a fine decoration illustrating an early locomotive hauling three chaldron waggons of coal. We can only surmise whether the maker was a locomotive driver or perhaps a colliery engineer.

Made by T. Crosby, 1854, Sheet brass
BM ref. 2001-105, 90 x 60mm (3¹/₂ x 2¹/₂in).)

A Wrought Iron Chimney Crane

In the 17th and 18th centuries, the large open hearth provided the main fireplace for cooking. Domestic ironwork was designed and made by the local blacksmith, who used his special skills to provide a piece of equipment both attractive and functional.

The chimney crane consisted of a large wrought iron bracket, suspended from the side of the fireplace, allowing the crane to swing in a quarter circle towards the fire. A pot hook could be slid along the main horizontal bar, enabling a cauldron to be moved over the fire at different levels, whilst another lever raised and lowered the pot hook, allowing for the finest of adjustments to be made.

Chimney Crane, Maker not known, Late 18th century
BM ref. 1995-8.2, 1250 x 1170mm (49 x 46in)

Tidy Betty
BM ref. 1972-161.2 ,
580 x 200 x 340mm ,
(23 x 8 x 13¹/₂ in)

Lover's Knot Fender and Tidy Betty

The blackness of the kitchen range contrasted with the hearth furniture, the fender, 'tidy betty', reckon bar and hooks, many of which were handmade from iron, and were kept brightly burnished. One such fender, with a matching 'tidy betty', (used to keep the ashes from sight), and poker stand was made by WILLIAM PATTISON CHISHOLM, (left) colliery blacksmith at Coxhoe colliery in Co. Durham. The top of the fender is made from one piece of iron with five 'plates', the largest and two smaller ones taking the shape of a 'true lover's knot' and the end ones, a pear design. Underneath are supporting pillars of wine glass shape. Even the screws are fashioned in the shape of acorns! The lover's knot pattern was a familiar design often used on quilts. William's wife, Sarah, was a fine needlewoman and a quilter and it is highly likely that one of her templates was used in the making of this fender, which was a wedding present to her from her husband. It took two years for William to complete, working in his spare time between 1892 and 1893, when they were married – a true labour of love!

Fender
BM ref. 1972-161.1,   1230 x 320 x 280mm (48¹/₂ x 12¹/₂ x 11 in)

38

Swan fender

The most superb example of craftsmanship demonstrated in a domestic item, this fender, from the Darlington area of County Durham, is certainly a work of art. Sadly little is known of the maker, one JOHN KEARTON, who has used such imagination and inventiveness in his design for this piece. It is quite likely that, with such skills, he may have worked for the North Road Locomotive Works, which were established in Darlington in 1863.

The really complex fretted design incorporates three umbrella type stands for pot or kettle, which can be raised or lowered to form frills illustrating oak leaves, and snowdrops. Swans, cut in fret, have been curved to follow the shape of the fender, whilst engine turned uprights give it strength. The whole fender, with its interlaced heart shaped highly polished leaves, demonstrates a quality of workmanship rarely seen in a piece of domestic hearth furniture.

Brass Kitchen Range

In the colliery villages of the North East of England, the hearth was the focal point of the home and family life centred around the coal-fired kitchen range, which provided heat, endless supplies of hot water for the pitman's bath and of course an oven for cooking. Fireside fittings and ornaments were outstanding features in miners' homes, and brass and copper have always been popular materials with which to adorn the hearth, whether it was in the form of candlesticks, trivets, tidies or brass animals. In the 19th century both materials were used extensively in heavy industry for engines, railway locomotives and machinery of all kinds. Sheet brass and boiler tubing were available in abundance and it must have been very tempting for a worker in the pit yard or shipyard to 'borrow' some left over bits and pieces to take home and make into something attractive with which to decorate the black kitchen range! The brass drying rail was often made from two lengths of brass pipe, joined in the middle by a ferule. The two lengths of pipe were the longest that could be secreted down the trouser leg, when walking out of the colliery yard! Nothing was wasted and works of art were created from scraps of brass, often specially inscribed and decorated – an excellent means of recycling.

This splendid model of a kitchen range was made by a shipbuilder on Tyneside, towards the end of the 19th century and represents one of the finest examples of traditional English brassware. Exceptional quality and workmanship are particularly well demonstrated in the use of both copper and brass in the parquetry of the hearth in imitation of a rag rug.

Model of a Kitchen Range, Late 19th century, Brass and Copper
BM ref. 2002-171.158, 380 x 325 x 375mm (15 x 12³/4 x 14¹/2 in)

Brass Comb Racks

Brass comb racks or tidies, as they were sometimes known, were much prized and would often be made as presents by the colliery engineer for his wife. They were made from left over pieces of sheet brass, bent into shape, cut, filed and soldered together, and were used for storing brushes and combs, pens and pencils, spills, matches and other odds and ends. The designs were pierced through the brass, which was sometimes inscribed with a pattern or date. The shape of a bird's beak was often used. Here birds and stags combine to form an attractive pattern.

BM ref. 1994-90.6, 240 x 160mm (9¹/₂ x 6¹/₄ in)

This comb rack is more unusual in that it depicts two unicorns, cut out from the brass supporting a round frame, surmounted by a crown and VR. The frame was probably intended for a photograph or picture. Traditionally two unicorns were used in the Scottish coat of arms and this may have been a present for someone of Scottish descent, during Queen Victoria's reign.

BM ref. 1995-93, 250 x 240mm (10 x 9¹/₂ in)

This comb rack was made from the brass of an engine involved in a railway accident at Otterington, near Thirsk on the North Eastern Railway on 2nd November 1892. A signalman's error caused the Edinburgh to London express to crash into a heavy goods train. Ten people died and 12 were injured. The tidy was made to commemorate the accident.

BM ref. 1995-71, 230 x 160mm (9 x 6¹/₄ in)

Trivet from North
East England
BM ref. 2002-171.99
233 x 145 x 28mm
(9 x 5³/₄ x 1in)

Brass Trivets

Domestic laundering irons of the simple flat type, sometimes known as 'sad' irons were heated in front of the fire and required a stand or trivet, between being heated and when not in use. Many trivets were supplied by the iron manufacturers in cast iron or cast brass, and sometimes home-made designs were copied from these. Smaller pieces of scrap sheet brass were saved from work to be taken home, carefully cut and filed, and made into an attractive design, incorporating hearts, flowers and scrolls. These trivets were often produced in pairs, and whether for use or ornament, they made an admirable gift for the wife.

Handmade trivets had a simple charm and individuality and when polished, they gleamed on the hearth. Templates for the designs were sometimes based on ordinary household objects, and patterns were often associated with a particular area, within the North East.

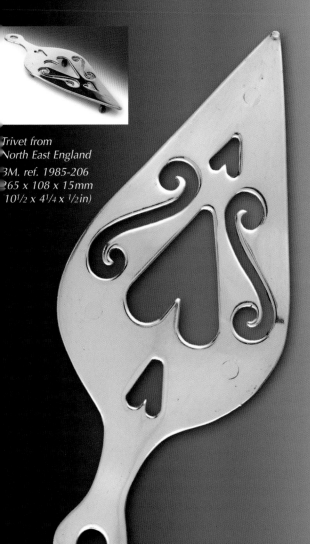

Trivet from
North East England
BM. ref. 1985-206
265 x 108 x 15mm
(10¹/₂ x 4¹/₄ x ¹/₂in)

Trivet from
North East England
*BM ref. 2002-
171.100*
307 x 142 x 39mm
(12 x 5¹/₂ x1¹/₂in)

Brass Animals

Stags and horses were the most popular animals to be made from sheet brass, and were often made in pairs to adorn a mantelpiece. Some were carefully engraved to emphasise detail whilst others were left in plain silhouette. Brass tube could be cut in half for the base.

Polar bear
BM ref. 2002-171.113
125 x 65mm (5 x 2¹/₂in)

Cow with horns (one of a pair)
BM ref. 2002-171.108
240 x 200mm
(8 x 4³/₄in)

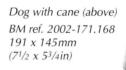

Dog with cane (above)
BM ref. 2002-171.168
191 x 145mm
(7¹/₂ x 5³/₄in)

Horse and Foal
BM ref. 2002-171.106
227 x 117mm (9 x 4³/₄in)

Horse (right)
BM ref. 2002-171.105
143 x 150mm
(5¹/₂ x 6in)

Stag (one of a pair) right
BM ref. 2002-171.110
195 x 100mm
(7³/₄ x 4in)

POTTERY AND GLASS

Sunderland Ware Jugs

ALTHOUGH THE POTTERY INDUSTRY on Tyneside and Wearside may date back to mediaeval times, our earliest records are from the 1700s. Many different types of pottery were produced, from the brown earthen wares used for cooking, the finer printed transfer cream wares to the purple and pink lustres. The Sunderland potteries became particularly well known for their lustre wares, often decorated with transfers of the Wearmouth Bridge, Masonic and Friendly Society symbols, and Maritime subjects with appropriate verses and mottoes. The jug (right) bears a transfer print of Giuseppe Garibaldi (1807-1882) the Italian patriot, who visited Newcastle in 1854, though the hand painted decoration and inscription of the coal waggon and pitman's tools is of more interest to us as a piece of folk art. The jug was possibly made at the Sunderland 'Garrison' pottery.

c. 1862, BM ref. 1994-224, 180 mm high (7in high)

The establishment of these local potteries was the result of the huge trade in coal, which was exported in ships from the rivers Tyne and Wear, returning with ballast in the form of china clay and flints. Lustre ware was produced on Tyneside as well as on Wearside. Sometimes the copper plates used for transfer designs were sold and exchanged between potteries and it is never easy to be sure where a particular piece originated.

This jug, c.1835, possibly commemorates a marriage. Hand painted in the form of an imaginary coat of arms, with a tree as the crest, it illustrates all the tools of the carpenter's trade.

c. 1835, BM ref. 2000-57, 230 mm high (9in high)

A Blacksmith's Salt Kit

Wherever there was suitable clay together with a supply of coal, the potteries of the North of England could provide the majority of earthenware cooking pots, storage jars, and baking dishes for domestic use, as well as novelty and commemorative pieces, such as puzzle mugs, frog mugs, tobacco jars, money boxes and bird whistles.

Many such potteries were established on Tyneside and Wearside, at Wetheriggs near Penrith, in Cumberland, around Halifax in West Yorkshire and at Burton in Lonsdale, each pottery developing its own speciality and style of decoration.

Salt jars, or salt kits as they were known, were most useful pieces of equipment in the kitchen. They kept the salt dry and clean, but at the same time allowed easy access to a handful of salt, which was in constant use for cooking and preserving. This delightful earthenware salt kit has been glazed and decorated with the tools of the blacksmith's trade, and bears the motto of the hammer men, 'with hamer in hand all arts doth stand'. It was made for the village blacksmith, Andrew Burtholme, at Banks Burn, Lanercost, near Brampton in Cumberland, in 1857. The jar bears his initials and models of his cat and dog sit on the top. Andrew was born in 1806, at nearby Irthington, and the salt kit had been passed down in the family. The glazes and decoration are unusual and have not been identified to a particular pottery.

c.1857, BM ref. 1986-46, 290mm (11½ in)

Slipware Pottery Chest of Drawers

Until recently very little was known about the pottery at Canney Hill near Bishop Auckland, Co. Durham, other than that it was established c.1840 and operated until 1913. This fine earthenware chest of drawers, from Canney Hill, has been built up from slabs of red clay, each of the drawers having been made, as a separate entity, to work. The whole has been carefully decorated with slip trailing and the drawers have their own spotted slip details. The chest of drawers is dated 1862 and it was reputed to have been made as an apprentice piece. All trace of the pottery at Canney Hill has now gone and we can only surmise what types of pottery were produced there other than earthenwares made in local clays. It is quite possible that some pottery was bought in from Staffordshire to be decorated locally for special orders.

c. 1862
BM ref. 1967-464,   240 x 245 x 120mm (9¹/₂ x 9³/₄ x 4³/₄in)

Slipware Cradle, Chair and Money Box

Miniature model cradles were being made in the potteries of Staffordshire in the 17th century, in imitation of the full size oak cradles in use at that period. From 1800, the fashion for making cradles had been adopted by the northern potteries. Usually with a hood and rockers, they were made to commemorate a child's birth or christening. Rocking chairs were also made and these sometimes bear a name and date. The cradles were often decorated with moulded birds, hens and chickens.

This cradle and rocking chair have been made in slabs of red and white clay to form 'agate' ware, and then have been slip decorated. They may have been made by one of the potteries on the Tyne or Wear, though very similar examples were made at Cliviger, near Burnley. Other novelties such as bird whistles and money boxes were also made in slipware.

Money Box (left) made by a potter from Burton in Lonsdale for James Whitaker, Headmaster of the Kendal Bluecoat School in 1838.
BM ref. 2002-171.79
230 x 93 mm
(9 x 3³/₄ in)

Cradle (left) c.1870
BM ref. 2008-11.1
290 x 170 x 230mm (11¹/₂ x 6³/₄ x 9in)
Rocking Chair (right) c.1864
BM ref. 2008- 11.2
140 x 110 x 180mm (5¹/₄ x 4³/₄ x 7in)

Tin tray covered with boody including part of a broken doll
BM ref. 1980-799, 420 x 340 mm (16$^1/_2$ x13$^1/_2$in)

Boody Pottery

The term 'boody' was well known in the dialect of Northumberland and Durham and referred to broken pieces of pottery or anything else which 'shines or glenters or lay glinting in the sunshine'. In 1897, Hobbies weekly magazine was instructing on 'china patchwork or mosaic'. Even at that time the magazine tells us that 'amateurs have been known to rake over suburban rubbish heaps, rejoicing at each dirty, but gaily coloured treasure that is unearthed.'

The sherds of pottery and porcelain were saved to be embedded into putty or similar, on tin plates, bottles and even drain pipes (for umbrella stands)! Wooden items were covered, such as mirrors and garden tables! Nothing was wasted and this early form of recycling produced some really decorative creations with which to adorn the home.

Boody pottery money box in the shape of a cottage
BM ref. 2002-171.67
217 x 148 x 244mm
(8$^3/_4$ x 5$^1/_2$ x 9$^1/_2$in)

Trench and Shell art

During and after the First World War, souvenirs from the battlefields, such as spent artillery shell cases, shrapnel and bullets were saved, and made into a new form of folk art which became known as Trench Art. With the most basic of equipment, and often in less than congenial circumstances, the soldiers engraved, punched and hammered to produce all manner of souvenirs, from vases, poker stands, cigarette cases and match box holders to gongs.

The plate (left) is a cross between boody pottery and trench art. It has been covered with putty into which has been set spent bullets, uniform buttons, badges from Durham and York regiments, as well as medals and coins.

BM ref. 1980-873, 260 mm (10¼in) diam

The tin plate (below) illustrates a variety of 'flotsam and jetsam', including badges, buttons, brooches and other small metallic items surrounded by small sea shells.

BM ref. 2002-171.66
310mm (12in) diam

One of a pair of shell cases, dated 1916 and 1917 (above) with embossed background and vine leaf decoration.

BM ref. 2008-12,
100 x 296 mm (4 x 11½in)

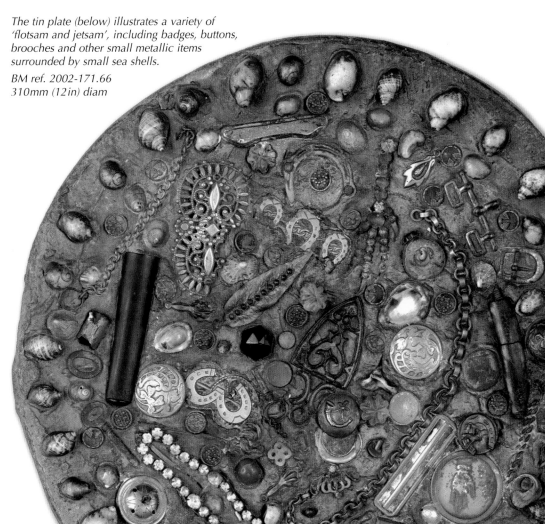

Cigar Label Plate

The smoking of cigars was a popular pastime for men during the 19th century, and it is said that Edward (later Edward VII) particularly enjoyed smoking cigars much to the displeasure of his mother Queen Victoria! Cigars were imported from South America, Brazil, Mexico and the USA. Cuban cigars were considered by many to be of the best quality.

Each cigar was carefully wrapped in a paper band. The cigars were then packed and stored in wooden boxes to maintain constant humidity. Inside the box lid was a colourful printed label featuring such scenes as Indian Chiefs, Buffalo Bill, Patriotic scenes, Biblical and Political subjects and Costumed Spanish beauties.

Cigar bands and box labels were quite prized and collected. Here they have been stuck on a plate surrounding a colourful and exotic scene, with a lady, supporting a banner declaring *Socialism*!

Collage plate, c.1910
BM ref. 1982-51, 250 x 200mm (9³/₄ x 8in)

Folk Art in Bottles

The tradition of making models in bottles seems to have begun in Europe in the early 1700s.

One bottle, made in 1719, by a German, one Matthias Buchinger, and containing mining scenes, was discovered in the collection at Snowshill Manor, in Gloucestershire. Whilst the making of ships and models in bottles has been documented, little is known about the Crucifixion and other ornamental examples found throughout the USA and Europe. We cannot be sure why the bottles were made and by whom, though they do exemplify amazing skill and craftsmanship and it is no surprise that some were called 'Patience bottles'!

The Crucifixion bottles are a potent symbol of the Christian faith, and in the North of England, were known, remembered and certainly in evidence in Roman Catholic households at Easter time, up until the 20th century. They have become known as 'God in a Bottle'! The crucifixes were made from small pieces of wood, which were jointed together, the cross being augmented with ladders, pincers, hammer and sponge. Once the construction of the crucifix had been completed, the bottle was filled with ordinary water, to expand the joints of the wood, and to hold the cross in place.

Some bottles, in the North, were made by Dominic Pannica, of Bishop Auckland, who came over from Southern Italy, to run an ice cream parlour. Other examples were made from wood and tassels in the shape of a Maltese cross, and some from the white pith supposedly from an elderberry tree.

'God in a Bottle' with label
'these tools are a replica of those used in making Dore and Chinley Railway Tunnel'
(let and right) late 1800s
BM ref. 2002-171.56
300 x 80mm (12 x 3¹/₄in)

Bottle with bobbins (above centre) North of England
BM ref. 2007-48, 300 x 100mm (12 x 4in)

Glass tankard in memory of the Hartley Colliery Disaster 16 January 1862, 204 lives lost

BM ref. 1976-846.1, 136 x 120mm (5¹/₄ x 4³/₄in)

Glass jug in memory of the West Stanley Disaster 1909 168 lives lost

BM ref. 1996-15.12 100 x 94mm (4 x 3³/₄in)

Sundae glass in memory of the Seaham Colliery Explosion Sept 8 1880, 164 lives lost

BM ref. 2007-150.1, 114 x 115mm (4¹/₂ x 4¹/₂in)

Colliery Disaster Glasses

The dangers of working deep down underground in the coal mines of the Great Northern Coalfield, have been well recorded. Most accidents were caused by explosions, but many were due to floods, carbon monoxide poisoning and roof falls. Hardly a year passed when there was no fatality and many stand out in history for the sheer numbers killed, with the consequent impact on the communities involved. It was as a direct result of certain disasters that working conditions in the coal mines were improved. After the 1812 Felling Disaster, Sir Humphry Davy constructed a 'safe' lamp. After the 1862 Hartley Disaster, legislation was brought in stipulating that every new pit to be sunk must have two shafts.

Relief Funds helped to raise money for the families involved, and souvenirs, such as commemorative booklets, printed sheets of verse and poetry, and paper serviettes were sold to support these funds. Souvenirs, in the form of cheap glass, were etched, possibly by market stall holders, commemorating the place and date of the disaster, and the number of lives lost. Little is known about the origin of these glasses, as to where they were made and who made them. Dated examples record disasters between 1844 and 1916, though the majority of the glasses seem to have been made between 1890 and the early 1900s. We do not know whether these pieces were made at about the time of a disaster or later as a token of remembrance. One glass jug records three different disasters dating between 1880 and 1909. By the time of the Easington Disaster in 1951, when 83 lives were lost, the custom seems to have died out, as no glasses appear to have been made.

Other Folk Art

Spar Ornaments

 N THE 19TH CENTURY, leadmining flourished in the North Pennines, particularly in Weardale and on Alston Moor, where the veins of lead were rich in minerals such as fluorspar, crystals of galena, quartz, calcite and pyrite. These colourful crystals were collected by the miners and were made into spar-boxes, grottoes and domes. Quite often mirrors and candles were used to enhance the natural sparkle of the crystals to great effect. One box was exhibited at the Great Exhibition in 1851, and in the late 1800s, exhibitions and competitions were held at local shows. The making of these wonderful pieces was largely restricted to the leadmining areas and as such, little has been written about them - they represent a much neglected form of north country folk art.

The dome (above) is made up of examples of fluorspar all collected from the Weardale area. The green crystals of fluorite are more unusual and came from only a few mines.

c. 1900, BM ref. 2001-86, 400 x 340mm (15³/₄ x 13¹/₂ in)

Coal and Ironstone Carvings

The art of carving on coal and ironstone, minerals in plentiful supply in the North of England, saw the production of many small pieces such as boots, shoes, crosses and bibles. As recently as the 1970s, the newspaper of the coal industry, Coal News, ran a competition for the best crown to be carved from coal, the crown to be presented to the winning team in the Triple Crown Rugby Union international series. Coal from West Cumberland and South and West Yorkshire, was ideal for this work as the coal was finely grained, and lent itself to this type of work. Regretfully few examples have survived.

Bible (left and below) with carving of St. Peter's Church, Stanley, near Wakefield on the reverse.
BM ref. 2002-171.40
62 x 17 x 90mm
(2¹/₂ x ¹/₂ x 3¹/₂ in)

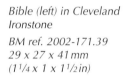

Bible (left) in Cleveland Ironstone
BM ref. 2002-171.39
29 x 27 x 41mm
(1¹/₄ x 1 x 1¹/₂ in)

Boot (right)
BM ref. 2002-171.164
80 x 54 x 22mm
(3 x 2¹/₄ x 1in)

Boot (left) in Cannel Coal, hollowed out to form a match holder
BM ref. 2002-171.41
103 x 38 x 62mm
(4 x 1¹/₂ x 2¹/₂ in)

Leatherwork Miner

Leather has traditionally been worked for a variety of crafts from tanning to saddlery and the making of boots and shoes. It was also used in the Victorian home for the making of decorative pictures and ornaments in the shape of fruit and flowers. This sculpture, however, is most unusual, in that it was obviously made as a decoration, though not for the home. It was discovered in the cellar of a pub in Durham and is thought to have been the work of a saddler at Browney Colliery, Co. Durham. The leather used probably consisted of off cuts and scrap pieces left over from the making of pit pony and horse harness. The maker must have had a fair knowledge of leatherwork as well as a good understanding of the life of a miner underground. The scene is most atmospheric. The colour of the miner's clothing contrasts with the blackness of the coal seam and the whole piece is evocative of another world.

Leather sculpture of pitman, Maker unknown, 20th century, Leather on plaster
BM ref. 2002-7, 920 x 770 x 100mm (36 x30 x4in)

John Wesley - Vertebra

The natural texture and interesting shape of bones, horns and antlers have inspired their adaptation into a wide variety of artefacts, both ornamental and useful. Cooking utensils, knife handles, musical instruments, gaming counters, jewellery, beakers, dosing horns, powder flasks, inlay for furniture, and walking sticks, to mention only a few, have all been crafted from these natural materials.

One of the most unusual ornaments has been made from the sixth vertebra of a heavy horse, such as a Shire or Clydesdale. The shape lends itself to the imagination, having been painted to represent a preacher, possibly the figure of John Wesley. The ball joint forms the head, whilst the front projections of the bone form the raised hands of the preacher from which his surplice falls. The back projections appear as his cassock!

Examples of this curious piece have been found in the North East of England, Yorkshire and Lincolnshire. Perhaps it was regarded as some kind of talisman.

Horse vertebra Wesley
Early 19th century
From Halifax area
6th vertebra bone of a heavy horse

BM ref. 2002-171.65
122 x 135 x 135mm
(4 3/4 x 5 1/4 x 5 1/4 in)

Scrimshaw powder flask, Maker not known, c.1850/60, Cow horn
BM ref. 2007-234 380mm (15 in) in length

Scrimshaw Powder Flask

SCRIMSHAW is generally the name that is given to carvings made, from the early 1800s, by whalers and seamen, on whale bone and whale teeth, and also on the tusks of walruses. It is also used for the carvings and decoration on other forms of horn and bone.

Cow and Ox horn was commonly used for the making of powder flasks. Horn was an ideal material for the purpose as it was light weight, tough and waterproof, and also being spark proof, was particularly suitable for carrying black powder used to load and fire the firearm. Moreover cow horn was not expensive as it was readily available from slaughter yards.

Simple tools were used to cut the design onto the surface, which would then be polished. Many were decorated with scenes or subjects of special note or commemorating particular events. This example has been carved with images of early locomotives, with some artistic licence! The Liverpool to Manchester Railway, opened in 1830, is featured with the loco *Rocket* hauling passenger carriages. Other locomotives illustrated are *Puffing Billy* and possibly *Samson, North Star* and *Jupiter*. Costumed figures probably date to the 1840/50s.

Animals from Bottle Tops

Crown corks or Crown caps as they are sometimes known, were invented for bottled carbonated beverages, in 1891 by one William Painter of Baltimore in the USA. They are used worldwide and the crown corks are widely collected, though many millions must be discarded every day. The growing emphasis on recycling has led to the creative use of much household rubbish, which would otherwise be discarded. During the latter part of the 20th century, there was a fascination for making something from nothing and these crown cork animals have become part of a new tradition. They can be made by anyone with the least of craft skills and they readily identify the part of the country or world that one is in!

Giraffe (above), 20th century
BM ref. 2003-74, 260 x 135 x 100 mm
(10 1/4 x 5 1/4 x 4 in)

Cat, 20th century
BM ref. 2002-171.179, 80 x 120 x 70 mm (3 1/4 x 4 3/4 x 2 3/4 in)

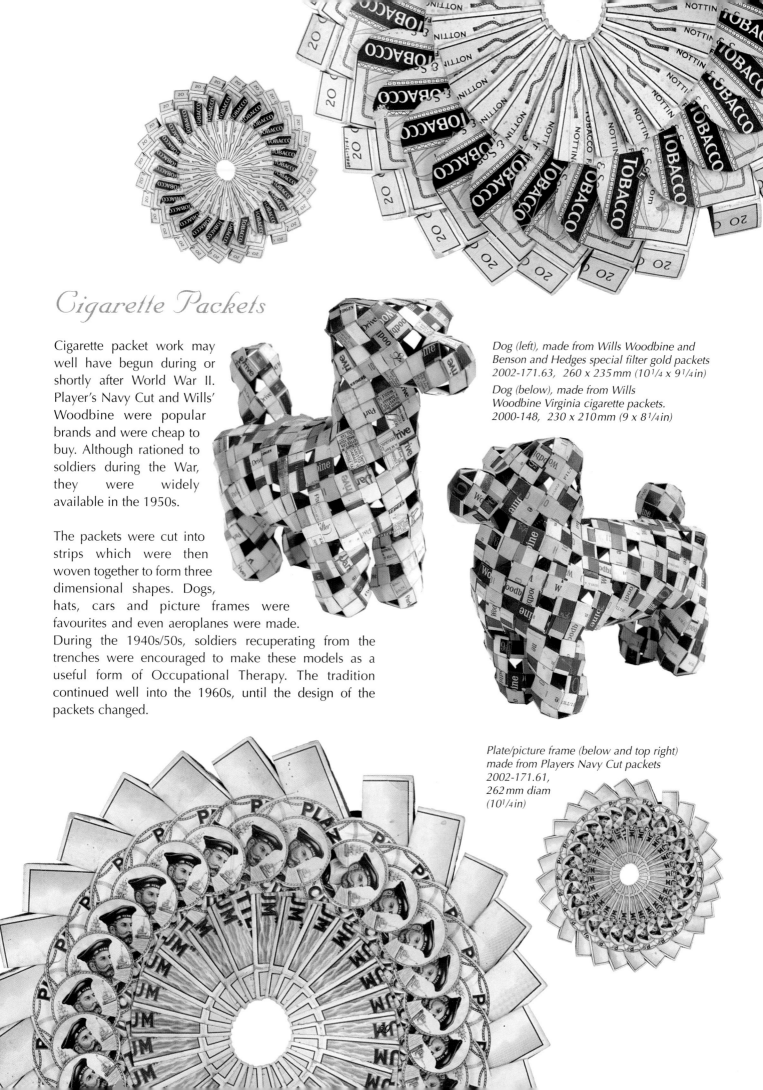

Cigarette Packets

Cigarette packet work may well have begun during or shortly after World War II. Player's Navy Cut and Wills' Woodbine were popular brands and were cheap to buy. Although rationed to soldiers during the War, they were widely available in the 1950s.

The packets were cut into strips which were then woven together to form three dimensional shapes. Dogs, hats, cars and picture frames were favourites and even aeroplanes were made.

During the 1940s/50s, soldiers recuperating from the trenches were encouraged to make these models as a useful form of Occupational Therapy. The tradition continued well into the 1960s, until the design of the packets changed.

Dog (left), made from Wills Woodbine and Benson and Hedges special filter gold packets 2002-171.63, 260 x 235mm (10¹/₄ x 9¹/₄in)

Dog (below), made from Wills Woodbine Virginia cigarette packets. 2000-148, 230 x 210mm (9 x 8¹/₄in)

Plate/picture frame (below and top right) made from Players Navy Cut packets 2002-171.61, 262mm diam (10¹/₄in)

Cut-Paper Work

The first half of the 18th century was the great period for the craft of paper-cutting. This vernacular craft continued in England well into the 19th century and was a popular pastime enabling ladies of leisure to demonstrate their artistic accomplishments. The craft has much in common with the shadow theatre and the painting of silhouettes, both in vogue in the Regency period.

This craft, however, required only the most basic of materials, employing scissors and paper of contrasting colours, usually white on a black background.

Subjects depicted included classical and biblical scenes, silhouettes of birds and animals as well as other features of natural history. As apparently knives were not used for this work, the scissors must have been amazingly sharp to cut such fine detail out of the paper. Sometimes the paper was pierced with holes or embossed to create an effect of relief. The work is extremely fine and must have demanded hours of patience to achieve a successful result.

Calligraphy

Calligraphy has been defined as the art of beautiful writing. The craft illustrates technical skills and can be both expressive and harmonious in its design. Often used for certificates, testimonials and memorial documents, the work has an individual and unique character. This pen and wash poster can certainly be regarded as unique! It was the work of one GEORGE ELLIOT, a patient in Bensham Lunatic Asylum, Gateshead in 1849. Depicting himself as 'Emperor of the World and Son of George the Fourth of Great Britain', it would appear that he suffered from delusions on a grand scale! The reverse of the poster gives detailed hand written instructions for the 'Building of the Imperial Palace of the True God, 1849'. George's artistry and penmanship skills are unquestionable, and one would have thought that this may have been the work of a typesetter or printer.

Calligraphy, George Elliot, 1849, Pen and wash
BM ref. 1985-308, 296 x 482mm (11¹/₂ x 19in)

Ship model

An imaginary model of a ship entitled H.M.S. Blake (right) with elaborate decoration of shells and small porcelain dolls - a glorious fantasy, was made by the gamekeeper at Beldon Hall, Yorkshire, c.1860-70.

BM ref. 1986-94,
660 x 480mm (26 x 19in)

Model Keelboat

From the 16th century onwards, the keelmen were of huge importance to the success of the coal trade. The keel boats, with their shallow draughts, could transport 8 Newcastle chaldrons of coal down the river Tyne to larger sea-going vessels which exported the coal to London and Europe. The keelmen ran their own societies and welfare organisations and for many years maintained a high degree of independence, though they, like the miners, had to enter into a yearly bond with their masters.

The model (right) was made, c.1900, by WILLIAM ROOTHAM, one of the last keelmen to live in the Keelmen's Hospital in Newcastle upon Tyne.

BM ref. 2003-174, 510 x 510mm (20 x 20in)

YORKSHIRE. LADY.
= THE. PROPERTY. OF. A. HEAP'S =
1932. 1st K.H.S. 11th GT. YORKSHIRE. AMAL. NEVERS.
1934. 1st K.H.S. 1st LEEDS & DIST. FED 3rd GT. YORKS. AMAL.
POITIERS

L. WADSWORTH

FURTHER READING

Allan, Rosemary E.
Quilts and Coverlets.
Beamish Museum, 2007

Allan, Rosemary E.
From Rags to Riches,
North Country Rag Rugs.
Beamish Museum, 2007

Ayres, James.
British Folk Art.
Barrie and Jenkins, 1977

Ayres, James.
English Naïve Paintings
1750-1900,
Thames and Hudson,
1980

Brears, Peter C.D.
English Country Pottery.
David and Charles, 1971

Brears, Peter C.D.
North Country Folk Art.
John Donald, 1989

Cooper, Emmanuel.
People's Art.
Mainstream Publishing,
1994

Glassie, Henry.
The Spirit of Folk Art,
New York, 1989

Gorman, John.
Bannner Bright.
Allen Lane, 1973.

Gorman, John.
Images of Labour.
Scorpion Publishing Ltd,
1985

Lambert, M. and Marx, E.
English Popular Art.
Batsford, 1951

**McManners, R. and
Wales, G.**
Shafts of Light, Mining Art
in the Great Northern
Coalfield.
Gemini Productions, 2002

Pinto, E.H.
Treen and Other Wooden
Bygones.
London, 1969

Tennant, Emma.
Rag Rugs of England and
America, Walker Books,
1992.

Young, Robert.
Folk Art.
Mitchell Beazley, 1999

PLACES TO VISIT
IN BRITAIN

American Museum in Britain,
Claverton Manor, Bath, BA2 7BD.
Tel. 01995 460503
www.americanmuseum.org

Beamish, The North of England Open Air Museum,
Beamish, County Durham, DH9 0RG.
Tel. 0191 370 4000
www.beamish.org.uk and www.beamishcollections.com

Compton Verney,
Compton Verney, Warwickshire, CV35 9HZ
Tel. 01926 645500
www.comptonverney.org.uk

St.Fagans National Museum History,
St.Fagans, Cardiff, CF5 6XB
Tel. 029 2057 3500
www.nmgw.ac.uk

York Castle Museum,
Castle Area, Eye of York, York, YO1 9RY
Tel. 01904 687687
www.york.trust.museum

Acknowledgements

FIRST AND FOREMOST, I would like to thank Peter Brears for his help and encouragement over the years. I am indeed greatly indebted to Peter, whose wonderful collection of North Country Folk Art, Beamish was able to acquire with the help of a Heritage Lottery Grant. Peter's collection complements the collections at Beamish, and together, they have provided the stimulus for this publication. Peter's book, *North Country Folk Art* is one of the few books on English Folk Art which looks in depth at the subject, and, incorporating Peter's amazing

knowledge on a multitude of subjects, is essential reading.

A special thanks go to Keith Bartlett at the Heritage Lottery Fund for enabling a grant to be made towards the purchase of Peter's collection, and also to Hannah Maddox, who worked diligently to secure funding for it.

I would like to thank the many people throughout the North of England, who have donated objects for the collections at Beamish over the last forty or more years. The material culture of this region is one of the richest in the British Isles and the Beamish collections reflect this. I have had the wonderful opportunity of being able to collect many of the objects illustrated in this book as well as of talking to and meeting many of the donors.

The Friends of Beamish have been hugely supportive and have helped to acquire objects, which would otherwise have been lost to the museum. Beamish would like to thank Renaissance North East, the Regional Museums Hub, who have grant aided the origination of this book, making its publication possible.

Such a wide variety of objects have presented their own problems in terms of photography and I am indeed most grateful for the trouble that has been taken by our gallant band of staff, both present and past, Justin Battong, Paul Castrey, Duncan Davis, Julian Harrop, and Jim Lawson for their excellent photographs. Paul Castrey has spent many hours working with the eye of a perfectionist. I would also like to acknowledge the photography of Eddie Ryle - Hodges, who worked with Beamish for a number of years.

Once again sincere thanks go to Ian C. Brown, for his patience and enthusiasm in designing this book. He has produced another superb and sensitive design which will inspire many in the much neglected subject of Folk Art.

As ever, my especial thanks must go to John Gall, who as past Deputy Director of Beamish, was responsible for the museum's development and historic authenticity. He has always given me the greatest advice and encouragement. His knowledge and appreciation of north eastern material culture and tradition is second to none!

MUSEUMS LIBRARIES ARCHIVES
PARTNERSHIP

Supported by
The National Lottery®
through the Heritage Lottery Fund

Heritage
Lottery Fund

RENAISSANCE
NORTH EAST
museums for
changing lives